by

# Rosalyn R. Walker

**Cause**

**I am without a cause**
**Free and unspoiled,**
**I am plain and me.**
**I am without a**
**Cause, yet, universal, and**
**Untamed, still I am free.**

ISBN: 0-7596-8408-1 (e-book)
ISBN: 0-7596-8409-X (Paperback)

This book is printed on acid free paper.

1stBooks - rev. 06/25/02

# ACKNOWLEDGEMENTS

I HAVE MANY THANKS TO FAMILY MEMBERS, FRIENDS AND COWORKERS WHOM I HAVE SUBJECTED MY THOUGHTS TO AT MOMENTS NOTICE. I REALLY THANK THEM FOR BEING AS PATIENT WITH ME WHETHER OR NOT THEY HAD THE TIME TO SPARE OR NOT. GOOD FAMILY AND FRIENDS ARE LIKE A GOOD GLASS OF WINE, AND A GOOD PAIR OF SHOES, HARD TO FIND.

SPECIAL THANKS TO MY FANTASTIC PARENTS WHOM NEVER STOPPED LISTENING BUT GAVE THEIR SUPPORT IN WHATEVER I DID. I DID BECOME SOMEONE BECAUSE THEY CARED ENOUGH TO STOP AND LISTEN AND GIVE ME GOOD ADVICE AND MOST OF ALL LET ME FALL AND PICK MYSELF UP WHEN I WAS SUPPOSED TO. I WISH THE WORLD HAD MORE PARENTS LIKE THEM TO HAVE SUPPORT FOR THOSE REAL DREAMS WHEN THOSE REAL DREAMS COME TRUE. I AM A REFLECTION OF MY PARENTS WHO GAVE ME SOME OF THEIR DREAMS AND ALLOWED ME TO HAVE DREAMS OF MY OWN.

BIG THANKS TO A LADY, A FRIEND AFAR, BUT BEST OF ALL, A TRUE BEST FRIEND. SHE GAVE DON'TS AND ME THE MOST IMPORTANT THINGS THAT ARE DO'S. IN MY COLLECTION I DEDICATE MY POEM FRIENDS TO MY DEAR FRIEND, PAMELA A.JONES.

TO MY TWO BEST COUSINS, GALE BONNER AND ROSE M. BONNER CALHOUN. YOU TWO ARE LIKE MY SISTERS AND I'LL ALWAYS LOVE YOU BOTH.

TO MY CHILDREN, YOU KNOW I LOVE YOU, ANDRÉ T. MARTIN, JR. AND ASHLEIGH CAONI JALIZA MARTIN. I LOVE YOU FROM THE EAST AND WEST AND FROM THE NORTH AND SOUTH AND INSIDE AND OUT, AND FROM THE TOP OF MY HEART TO THE BOTTOM OF BOTTOM OF HEART BECAUSE YOU ARE MY TWO BEST LINKS, AS I AM THE LINK FROM MY MOM AND DAD.

MOST OF ALL I'D LIKE TO ALWAYS THANK MY LORD AND SAVIOR BECAUSE ALL OF THIS WOULD HAVE NO MEANING IF HE HADN'T GIVEN ME A MIND TO KEEP WRITING THIS DOWN AND HAVING FAITH IN HIM AND IN MYSELF. PATIENCE IS VIRTUE. PATIENCE IS BEING BLESSED.

ROSALYN RENEE WALKER

| | |
|---|---|
| MARITAL STATUS: | DIVORCED |
| PAST TIME: | WRITING POETRY, CRAFTS, FLORAL ARRANGING AND BINGO, BINGO!!!!! |
| CHILDREN: | ANDRÉ THEODORE, JR., AND ASHLEIGH CAONI JALIZA MARTIN |
| PARENTS: | WILLIAM FRANK WALKER AND BERTHA MAE BONNER WALKER |
| SISTER: | DENISE HARRIS (I LOVE YOU ALWAYS) |
| NIECE/NEPHEW: | ADRIENNE AND TROY HARRIS |

# CONTENTS

# ENCHANTED

IT'S NO WONDER WHY I KEEP YOU NEAR MY HEART.
LIKE FIRE WORKS ON A FOURTH OF JULY,
I AM ALWAYS ENCHANTED BY YOUR PRESENCE.
LIKE THE WATERS ON A BEAUTIFUL ISLAND,
YOUR HEART IS SO CLEAR
THAT I CAN SEE RIGHT THROUGH IT AND
THAT'S A GOOD THING, BECAUSE I HOLD YOU
NEAR MY HEART,
AND THAT'S A GOOD HEART,
FULL OF LOVE,
FULL OF LIFE,
SO ENCHANTING,
LIKE FIRE WORKS ON A FOURTH OF JULY,
IT'S NO WONDER WHY I KEEP YOU NEAR MY HEART.

# I AM

I WALK THROUGH THIS LIFE AS A WOMAN, BUT DO YOU REALLY
SEE ME AS A WOMAN OR EVEN A WOMAN YOU RESPECT?
DO YOU OOH AND AAH BECAUSE MY HIPS ARE CURVED
AND SHAPED LIKE SHIPS IN CALM WATERS? I'M LOOKING
AT YOU, LOOKING AT ME, YOUR EYES THEY GAZE ALL OVER ME
BECAUSE MY WALK IS WITH SUCH GRACE AND MY BALANCE
WITH STYLE, I AM FLOATING IN RYTHYM LIKE THE WINDS BLOWING
FROM SIDE-TO-SIDE. MY SKIN IS DARK AND RICH IN COLOR,
BUT WHEN YOU LOOK UP AND SEE THAT MY SKIN IS DARK AND MY
HAIR IS NOT LONG, DO YOU DISRESPECT ME BY SAYING, DAMN?
MY HAIR IS NOT LONG, BUT IT'S AS SOFT AS A FEATHER. MY WALK,
LIKE LIGHT FEET, MY MIND FREE LIKE THE WINDS, AND THE
LOVE IN MY HEART IS AS WIDE AS THE OCEAN, DEEP AS THE SEA,
AND BRIGHT AND COLORFUL LIKE A SUNNY SPRING DAY.
A SMILE IN MY MIND, BODY AND SOUL, MY WORDS,
THEY BELONG ONLY TO ME, THEY ARE MINE NOT YOURS. STILL,
I AM A WOMAN WHOSE WALK IS FULL, FULL IN RESPECT, THAT

EVEN YOU CANNOT DENY ME MY RIGHTS.  I AM A WOMAN WITH
WORDS OF CONVICTION NOT DESTRUCTION, I AM A WOMAN OF GLADNESS
NOT SADNESS. I WALK WITH A SMILE, MY LIFE IS IN TUNE
AND MY SOUL FULL OF GLADNESS.  I AM A WOMAN THAT'S
MENTALLY AS STRONG AS TEN MEN IN STRENGTH
AND NOT EVEN YOU CAN KEEP ME DOWN.

# MOTHER, GRAND MOTHER, AND GREAT GRAND MOTHER

A VERY SPECIAL LADY YOU HAVE BEEN
DEEP INSIDE ME YOU'LL ALWAYS BE.
A SMILE I WILL HAVE IN REMEMBERING YOU,
AND WITH ALL THE LOVE WE SHARED.
I WILL NOW SAY GOOD BYE.
GOODBYE MOTHER,
GOODBYE GRAND MOTHER,
GOODBYE GREAT GRAND MOTHER,
I LOVED YOU SO DEAR, LIKE SO MANY OTHERS,
AND NOW YOU HAVE LEFT OUR PRESENCE,
BUT, NOT OUR HEARTS.
SLEEP MOTHER, SLEEP PEACEFULLY,
SLEEP GRAND MOTHER, SLEEP WITHOUT PAIN,
SLEEP GREAT GRAND MOTHER, SLEEP FREE AND
WITHOUT SUFFERING.
IN ANOTHER TIME WE WILL MEET AGAIN,
BUT NOW I MUST SAY GOOD BYE.

## A PORTRAIT OF A MEMORY

I AM THE MEMORIES OF A BREEZE BLOWN BY.
I AM A PORTRAIT OF A MEMORY ON A HOT AND COOL
BREEZY NIGHT.
I AM NOT THE BREEZE THAT YOU DREAMDT ABOUT.
I AM THE DREAM THAT YOU HAVE LIVED,
I AM THE DREAM OF ALL DREAMS AND
THE BELIEF THAT REAL DREAMS DO COME TRUE.
THE TRUE VISION OF ONE THOUSAND AND ONE
DREAMS
THAT ANY ONE MAN COULD DREAM.
I AM THE WHISPERING PORTRAIT OF ONE THOUSAND
AND ONE-SWEET MEMORIES BLOWN BY.

# STANDING HERE

I'M JUST STANDING HERE ADMIRING THE BEAUTY
THAT
SURROUNDS ME.
THOUGH ONE DAY THESE EYES WILL DRAW WEARY
AND
WON'T BE ABLE TO STAY OPEN,
I'LL JUST STAND HERE NOW AND ADMIRE THE
BEAUTY
THAT SURROUNDS ME.
I'M JUST LOOKING AT THE PEOPLE, THEY SEEM TO
HAVE
LAUGHTER TODAY AND THE SUNDAY DRIVERS,
THEY'RE LIKE OBJECTS STANDING HERE BESIDE ME.
I'M JUST STANDING HERE ADMIRING THE BEAUTY
THAT'S SURROUNDING ME.
THE MAN OVER THERE THAT'S CURSING, I SURE HOPE
THAT HE CAN READ MY MIND AND MAYBE HE, TOO,
WILL
COME STAND BESIDE ME AND THEN HE, TOO, CAN
ADMIRE
THE BEAUTY THAT SURROUNDS ME.

# CAUTION

FIRST LOVES ARE ALWAYS LIKE, GO STRAIGHT TO CAUTION, AND WHEN

YOU GET THERE, FIND NO ONE TO BLAME, BUT YOURSELF…

YOU SAW IT THERE FIRST, BUT WERE AFRAID TO CAPTURE THE
MOMENT. LOVE, LIKE TRUTH, KNOWS NO ONE, OPEN YOUR HEART AND SOMETIMES WHEN YOU MUST, LET IT BEAT FOR ITSELF.

## MS. RIGHT/MRS. WRIGHT

SPEAK WORDS UNTOLD, ONE DAY YOU WILL WANT
TO SAY
ALL THOSE WORDS, ALL THE WORDS THAT YOU
SAVED FOR
MS. RIGHT.
WELL, MS. RIGHT AIN'T JUMPING OUT OF A
MAGAZINE,
SO ZOOM YOUR ASS RIGHT BACK DOWN TO EARTH.
THIS
IS MARS TALKING TO PLUTO,
GET YOUR ASS BACK DOWN TO EARTH.
I'M THAT EVERY DAY WOMAN THAT YOU AREN'T
LOOKING
FOR, AND I TOO HAVE PROBLEMS.
I WON'T TOTE MINE AROUND LIKE LUGGAGE, I'LL
DEAL WITH
MINE THE BEST I KNOW HOW. I DON'T WANT YOURS
BECAUSE MINE IS ALREADY HEAVY ALL BY ITSELF.
I CAN LISTEN TO YOUR GARBAGE LIKE YOU CAN
LISTEN TO MINE.
BUT DON'T EXPECT ME TO LISTEN ATTENTIVELY,
AND TAKE
YOUR SHIT BACK WITH ME.. HOW DARE YOU!
JUST LEAVE THAT SHIT AT THE FRONT DOOR,
NOT MINE, AND LET'S JUST BE HAPPY. THAT'S H A P
P Y,
HAPPY TOGETHER. AND WHEN YOU WANT TO SPEAK
UNSPOKEN WORDS,
I'LL SHOW YOU MY LUGGAGE AND YOU CAN DO THE
SAME.
BUT, WHEN WE CLOSE OUR FRONT DOOR, WE'LL LIVE
HAPPILY
EVER AFTER. NOW, I'M MRS. WRIGHT!!!!

# FAR IS FAR

HOW FAR MUST ONE GO?
FAR, MUST ONE GO, MUST ONE GO TO DEPTHS.
MUST ONE SEE THE OTHERSIDE OF NOW WHERE?
MUST ONE CRY, BUT NOT WEEP, DIE, BUT NEVER
HAVE LIVED.

## YOUR LOVE

I CAN REMEMBER THE FIRST TIME, BUT ONLY WAS IT TILL
THE FIRST TIME WE HAD MADE LOVE.
IT WAS NOTHING THAT I HAD EVER HAD, BUT IT WAS THE BEST I HAD EVER HAD.
FOR THE FIRST TIME I HAD MADE LOVE.

# LOVING

LOVE LIKE TRUTH KNOWS NO ONE TO SPARE. OPEN YOUR HEART AND SOMETIMES WHEN YOU MUST, LET IT BEAT FOR ITSELF.

# A SMILE

A SMILE THAT CAPTURES ONE, ONE THAT CAN
BE TREASURED WITHIN ONE'S SELF FOR A LIFETIME.
SMILES ARE MADE UP OF SO MANY GRAND COLORS.
COLORS THAT WE CAN SEE WITHIN OUR HEARTS.
SMILES CAN ALMOST BE THAT OF LIFE OR DEATH.
JUST ONE SMILE TO MAKE THE DIFFERENCE,
BECAUSE IT SHOWS SOMEONE YOU REALLY CARE.

# ROUGHAGE OF A DIAMOND

YOU'RE LIKE A DIAMOND WAITING IN THIS LIFETIME
TO SPARKLE.
BRIGHT AND WITH SUCH BRILLANCE YOU'RE LIKE A
DIAMOND IN
THE ROUGHAGE. I'M NOT AFRAID TO TAKE YOUR
HAND, AND
I'M NOT AFRAID TO TAKE YOUR HAND IN MINE.
LOVE, LIKE TRUTH IS BLINDING IN THIS ROUGHAGE
AND
HAS OPENED ITS BEAUTY FOR YOU AND I TO SEE.
YOU ARE A SPARKLE THAT'S A DIAMOND, THAT'S
BRIGHT,
THAT'S BRILLIANT, AND VIBRANT WAITING IN A
LIFETIME
FOR A LIFE TIME TO SPARKLE.
SO SPARKLE LIKE A DIAMOND BECAUSE A DIAMOND
FOR MY LIFETIME YOU TRULY ARE.

# BLESSED

GOD BLESSED ME, HE BLESSED ME ALL OF MY LIFE.
THEN HE GAVE TO ME A SPECIAL LITTLE GIFT,
HE GAVE TO ME, YOU.
SO SMALL, SO MANY SMILES, SO MUCH LOVE AND SO MUCH
ME IN YOU AND THAT'S WHY I TRULY
LOVE YOU.

# WE CAME

WE CAME WITH DISTANCE.
HOW FAR, WE DIDN'T KNOW.
BUT A CHANCE, WE TOOK IT AND LIKE A LOT OF LIVES,
WE TOOK THE GOOD AND THE BAD, THE SUCCESS, THE FAILURES,
THE GROWTHS AND THE SET BACKS.
AND WITH ALL THAT'S HAPPENED, WE CAN STILL FIND LOVE.

## MINE TO GIVE

MY LOVE IS MYSTICAL, MY LOVE IS MAGICAL.
IT IS MY LOVE THAT BLENDS WITHIN YOUR HEART,
WITHIN MINE. A LOVE THAT MUST BE
SHARED AS TWO, AS INDIVIDUALS,
BUT TOGETHER AS A WHOLE.
WHO BUT US SHALL KNOW THE GROWTH.
LIKE SO MANY, LIKE A FLOWER THAT BLOOMS SO DOES
OUR LOVE, UNDERSTANDING, OUR TRUST.
LOVE IS LOVE, BUT MINE IS A VERY SPECIAL LOVE.
MYSTICAL, MAGICAL,
IT IS MY KIND OF LOVE,
MINE TO GIVE.

# FEELINGS

JUST IMAGINE GETTING HIT OVER THE HEAD WITH
ALL THIS SO-CALLED LOVE. YOU FIND YOURSELF
ACCUMULATING HEADACHEDS LIKE BILLS,
YOU FIND YOURSELF DRAINING, LIKE A BANK
ACCOUNT.
YOU GOT A TERRIBLE FEELING AND YOU DON'T
KNOW WHY.
YOU THOUGHT IT WAS LOVE, BUT YOU KNOW LOVE
SURE AS HECK AIN'T LIKE THIS.
YOU STOP AND WONDER WHY?

# A LOVE SEEN

A LOVE SEEN ON A SUNRISE AND A SUNSET TO A
RYTHYM THAT RHYMES.
WE CREATED A LOVE SCENE TO LAST FOREVER....
AND WE KISSED EACH OTHER'S LIPS A THOUSAND
TIMES,
BUT, IT WASN'T UNTIL NOW THAT WE KISSED FOR
THE FIRST TIME.
EVERYTHING IN MY HEART BEAT FOR THE FIRST
TIME, AND YOUR KISS,
HOW COULD I HAVE KISSED YOUR LIPS A THOUSAND
TIME AND THIS
KISS FEEL LIKE THE FIRST TIME THAT I KISSED YOUR
LIPS AND YOU
KISSED MINE.
NO ONE EVER TOLD ME THAT THEY WOKE UP TO A
LOVE SCENE,
BUT EARLY THIS MORNING, I WOKE TO A LOVE
SCENE.
AS THE SUN ROSE AGAINST YOUR LOVELY FACE,
THAT'S WHEN I KNEW I LOVED YOU FOREVER...
I KISSED YOUR LIPS A THOUSAND TIMES, IT WASN'T
UNTIL
NOW THAT THIS TIME WAS THE FIRST TIME.
AND IN THE MIDST OF CREATING A LOVE SCENE
AS THE SUN SETS LOVE BEGINS.

# TODAY

TODAY AND EVERY DAY, I'M GOING TO LOVE YOU,
AND YOU, MY SISTERS AND BROTHERS.
IT WASN'T YOU THAT DIED ON THE CROSS, IT WAS
JESUS WHO DIED ON THE CROSS, SO THAT YOU AND
I COULD LOVE FREELY.
I'M GOING TO LOVE YOU, YOU, YOU, AND EVEN YOU,
EVEN IF YOU DON'T WANT ME TO.
BUT IF IT'S YOU THAT CONCLUDES MY MESSAGE, IT'S
YOU THAT WON'T STAND TO THE END OF ALL TIMES.
LOVE, HOW CAN YOU EVER DENY IT, IT IS LOW COST,
IT'S AFFORDABLE, IT'S REALLY FREE AND IT'S
INCLUSIVE.
SO I'LL SAY ONE MORE TIME TO YOU MY SISTER AND
MY
BROTHER, I'M GOING TO LOVE, YOU, YOU, YOU, YOU
AND EVEN
YOU, EVEN IF YOU DON'T WANT ME TO.

# THE CONTENTS OF A JOURNEY

I WAS ON A JOURNEY AND IN SO MUCH PAIN WHEN I HEARD
THE WHISPERING AND ALMOST SILENT WORDS OF PEACE
FALL UPON MY EARS. ALL OVER MY BODY BECAME STILL AND
HE WHISPERED THE PAIN AND SUFFERING AWAY. THAT'S
WHEN I KNEW MY JOURNEY HERE, WAS OVER.
THERE IS NO WAY TO KNOW THE LENGTH OF ONE'S JOURNEY HERE,
BUT IT S THE CONTENTS OF ONE'S LIFE, THE BOUQUET OF LOVE
THAT SURROUNDS EVERYTHING YOU HAVE DONE AND SEEN
THAT WILL MAKE YOUR JOURNEY GREAT UNTIL THE END.
SO DRY YOUR TEARS, BECAUSE IF HE WOULD HAVE
TOLD YOU WHEN I WAS LEAVING, IT WOULD HAVE BEEN TOO MUCH
FOR YOU TO BEAR. THE LORD HAS BEEN SO GOOD TO ME,
HE HAS BLESSED ME ALL THROUGH MY JOURNEY BY
HOLDING MY HAND SO I COULD HOLD YOURS. THERE WILL ALWAYS
BE A SPECIAL LOVE BETWEEN US THAT WILL NEVER LEAVE OUR
HEARTS, OR MINDS. LOVE, YOU NEVER LOOSE IT, NOT EVEN IN
THE END OF ONE'S JOURNEY.

## WORKING TOGETHER

WORKING TOGETHER ACCOMPLISHES A LOT OF THINGS NOT YET IMAGINED AND HELPS DREAMS BECOME REALITY.

## PEACE

WHEN I CLOSED MY EYES
MY HAND WAS IN HIS HAND
AND HE GAVE ME PEACE
WHEN HE GAVE ME PEACE
I CLOSED MY EYES FOREVER IN THIS WORLD,
AND WALKED WITH HIM IN HIS WORLD
HE THEN GAVE ME REST.
MY SOUL, IT BELONGS TO GOD NOW
SO DON'T WORRY ABOUT ME
I'M AT HOME.
I'VE LEFT A LOT OF LOVE BEHIND,
I'VE LEFT A LOT OF MEMORIES AND
I ALWAYS KNEW YOU ALL LOVED ME,
BUT,
GOD LOVED ME BEST.

# COLOR ME WITH COLORS OF BEAUTY

COLOR ME WITH A BEAUTIFUL PICTURE BEFORE YOU CAST ME OUT.
I HAVE DREAMS, AND I HAVE DREAMDED OF MANY COLORS THAT
BLEND SO WELL THAT YOU AND I WOULD THINK WE WERE
RAINBOWS THAT ARE SO HIGH ABOVE THE CLOUDS IN THE SKY.
SO COLOR BLIND THIS DIRTY OLE WORLD WITH PAINTED
PICTURES OF BEAUTY BECAUSE THESE PAINTED BEAUTIES ARE OF YOU AND I.

## FREEDOM

FREEDOM COMES BUT ONCE IN THIS LIFETIME..
IT WILL COME WHEN THE SPIRIT DETACHES FROM THE WORN OUT
AND TIRED BODY. BUT WHILE ON THIS EARTH, STRUGGLES
ARE MORE AND OFTEN IN GOD'S WORLD THAN YOU THAT ARE
NOT AND WITHOUT. A STRUGGLE AND A DREAM FOR ALL OF GOD'S PEOPLE,
A STRUGGLE AND A DREAM RIGHT DOWN TO THE LAST BREATH, I'LL TAKE ONE DAY.
BUT, FREEDOM WILL BE MINE AND YOURS AND THE PLACE, THE PLACE
WILL BE WELL PREPARED. IN THE LAST DAYS THAT WE STRUGGLE, THE CAUSE
IS WELL WORTH IT, AND HIS PAYMENT WILL BE WELL DESERVED, BUT TOGETHER
WE WILL MAKE IT, AND WE'LL ALL BE TOGETHER.

# A MELODY

NEAR AND FAR I DID NOT IMAGINE YOU.
HERE AND NOW YOU ARE STANDING RIGHT BEFORE ME.
WATCHING AND WAITING YOUR LIKE A LOVE NOTE THAT'S COME TO
PLAY AND SET MY LOVE SOUL ON FIRE.
IN THE SUNSET FOR THIS MOMENT, I WANT TO
LAY HERE QUIETLY AND BE!
I'LL WAIT LIKE A STRING OF MELODIES THAT
ARE AS BEAUTIFUL AS PETALS ON A ROSE, ONE
FLOWER THAT HAS HALF-BLOOMED. I'LL WAIT
AND AS THE SUNLIGHT STROKES EACH
PETAL AND EACH PETAL BECOMES MORE
BEAUTIFUL I'LL WAIT FOR YOUR WARM EMBRACE
AS THE SUNLIGHT EMBRACES
US TOGETHER AND THE TOUCH, YOUR TOUCH,
SENDS EACH PETAL INTO FULL BLOOM.
NEAR AND FAR IN THE SUNLIGHT, I'LL REMAIN
HERE AND NOW IN THE SUNSET, YOURS FOREVER.

## NEAR AND FAR

NEAR AND FAR,
HERE AND NOW,
WATCHING AND WAITING
IN THE SUNSET
I'LL WAIT LIKE
PETALS ON A ROSE,
I'LL WAIT
FOR YOUR WARM EMBRACE
NEAR AND FAR,
HERE AND NOW.

## HAPPY BIRTHDAY TO YOU!

I HEARD THE BIRDS CHIRPING,
THEY HAD LOTS OF JOY AND LOVE IN THEIR VOICES.
THEN I STOPPED TO LISTEN TO THE BEAUTIFUL
SOUNDS AND
THEY WERE SINGING HAPPY BIRTHDAY TO YOU.
LET TODAY, THAT THE BIRDS SING A SONG TO YOU
BE AS LOVELY AS YOU ARE TO ME.
LET IT BE ALL DAY LONG THAT THE WORDS SING
OUT LOUD.   LIKE THE BIRDS CHIRPING LET
THEM SAY OUT LOUD, HAPPY BIRTHDAY TO YOU.

## A FLOWER

LIKE A FLOWER THAT BLOOMS WHEN A MOTHER
RAPS HER
LOVING ARMS AROUND HER CHILD, HER CHILD WILL
ALWAYS
FEEL A RADIANCE THAT IS SO PURE AND WARM.
THE BEAUTY AND HER FRAGRANCE THEY CAPTURE
WHAT GOD
HAS BLESSED A DAUGHTER TO HAVE.
A MOTHER SO DEAR,
A MOTHER TO CALL HER OWN,
BUT MOST OF ALL
A MOTHER THAT SHARES HER LOVE
ALL ON HER OWN.

## A BIRTHDAY WISH

TODAY IS A SPECIAL DAY, IT'S YOUR DAY
AND ITS MY DAY TO WISH YOU ALL THE
HAPPINESS YOU DESERVE.
SO HAPPY BIRTHDAY,
TO MY #1 MOM AND
HAPPY BIRTHDAY TO THE BEST MOM.
ALL DAY IS YOUR DAY, TODAY,
SO HAVE A

HAPPY
HAPPY
HAPPY

HAPPY BIRTHDAY TODAY!

LOVE ALWAYS,

ALWAYS, ALWAYS,

ALWAYS, ALWAYS,

YOUR DAUGHTER.

## GRANDMA

GRANDMA!

LOTS OF LOVE,

LOTS OF KISSES,

LOTS OF LOVE AND KISSES AND MANY

WONDERFUL WISHES TO MY GRANDMA
ON THIS LOVELY DAY, BUT NOT AS LOVELY AS YOU.
HAVE A GREAT DAY ON YOUR BIRTHDAY TODAY.

LOVE YA GRANDMA

ALWAYS ALWAYS ALWAYS

# FRIENDS

FAR BUT STILL BEST FRIENDS.
PLAIN PEOPLE CAN'T SEE FAR, THEY NEVER SEE THINGS TO REMINISCE ABOUT.
PEOPLE LOOK AND SEE, BUT PLAIN PEOPLE SEE PLAIN THINGS.
TRUE FRIENDS ARE ONE IN TEN THOUSAND AND NO MATTER WHAT PEOPLE SAY
OR DO, WE ARE STILL BEST FRIENDS.
THE FUN AT 13, THE EXCITEMENT BEING 16 AND TEARS OF JOY AT 18 AND
THE YEARS APART, GUESS WHAT, WE ARE STILL BEST FRIENDS.
AT OUR AGE THE YEARS WILL COME AND AT THIS AGE 37,
THERE WILL COME NUMBERS LIKE 38, 39, AND 40, BUT 13, 16 AND 18,
FUN, EXCITEMENT AND JOY, I SEE THIS
COMING AGAIN,
I SEE US ALWAYS BEING BEST FRIENDS.

## A CALM VOICE

DON'T GO TOO FAR
BECAUSE
I MIGHT NEED YOU TO BE NEAR ME.
I MIGHT NEED A GENTLE VOICE TO CALM ME IN WHOLE, I MIGHT NEED TO HAVE A WORD OR TWO THAT'S AS SWEET AS PURE CANE SUGAR, TRUE LIKE WORDS SPOKEN FROM THE TIPS OF A VIRGIN'S TONGUE.
DON'T LEAVE JUST YET, BECAUSE IT'S A BEGINNING ENERGIZED BY NO ENDING. I AM LOOKING FOR YOU AND I.

## SOUL- MATE OR CELL-MATE?

IF YOU SPEND A LIFETIME SEARCHING FOR A SOUL-MATE,
THEN HE OR SHE JUST MIGHT PASS YOU BY. THE MATE OF
YOUR SOUL IS FOUND WITHIN. YOU HAVE TO GO DEEP INSIDE YOURSELF
FOR THE FIRST CONNECTION AND IF YOU STAND STILL LONG ENOUGH, YOU'LL
FEEL AND KNOW HE OR SHE IS NEAR.
PEOPLE WHOM LIKE WHAT THEY SEE ON THE INSIDE OF THEMSELVES QUICKLY
IGNITE WHEN THEY FIND SOMEONE THAT'S DONE THE SAME.
LOOKING FOR ALL THE QUALITIES THAT ARE PERFECT IN A PERSON COULD BE ALL
THE WRONG QUALITIES IN A PERSON! ARE YOU SURE YOUR LOOKING FOR SOUL-MATE OR
HAVE YOU FOUND YOURSELF A CELL-MATE.
SOMETHING'S LAST FOR A LITTLE WHILE, SOMETHING'S A LIFETIME, AND
SOMETHING'S ARE LOST FOREVER.
A SOUL- MATE OR A CELL- MATE?
IT'S ON YOU!

## WINGS

FLY WITH WINGS THAT SPREAD AND FLY WAY UP.
WHILE OTHERS ARE SO OBVIOUS, THEY ONLY SEE LOOKING OUT.
DON'T LOOK BACK, LOOKING AT THEM, YOU MIGHT STAND STILL TOO.
SO SPREAD YOUR WINGS WAY UP AND FAR, DON'T STOP UNTIL THE TOP.
THE THINGS YOU HAVE THAT ARE MATERIAL, THEY WEAR AND TEAR AND
SOON FADE AWAY. THE THING MOST YOU'LL WANNA FIND WILL BE REAL
AND COMPLIMENT YOUR WHOLE LIFE BEING.
WINGS SPREAD, WINGS FLY WAY UP,
SO DON'T STOP ALONG THE WAY TRYING TO BE LIKE OTHERS BECAUSE YOU, TOO
MAYBE STANDING OVER THERE LOOKING OUT.

# A MENTION AWAY AND A FOOTSTEP TO WALK

JESUS IS JUST A MENTION AWAY AND A FOOTSTEP TO WALK.
EVEN BEFORE THE TROUBLE BEGINS, HE IS STANDING IN YOUR
TROUBLED TIMES.
HE IS FIGHTING FOR OUR SOULS SO WHY CAN'T YOU FIGHT FOR
HIS SPIRIT AND LOVE. CAN YOU CALL ON JESUS BEFORE
THE TROUBLE BEGINS? BUT, WILL YOU CALL ON JESUS
AFTER THE TROUBLE BEGINS? YOU OUGHT TO GET DOWN ON YOUR KNEES AND THANK HIM.
YOU NEED TO LET HIM BE A FRIEND WAY BEFORE THE TROUBLE
BEGINS AND WHEN THE TROUBLE BEGINS, IF YOU CALL ON JESUS
AND TRULY BELIEVE, THEN YOU WILL ALWAYS KNOW HE'LL NEVER
LEAVE YOU FALLING AND STANDING ALONE.
JESUS IS JUST A MENTION AWAY, AND A FOOTSTEP TO WALK, HE IS WITH YOU
IN ALL YOUR TIMES BEFORE THE TROUBLE BEGINS.
THOUGH YOU DIDN'T DO EVERYTHING YOU COULD DO FOR HIM, HE NEVER
STOP DOING EVERYTHING FOR YOU.
WHEN YOU THOUGHT THAT EVERYTHING YOU WERE DOING HAD MEANING
AND JOY, DIDN'T YOU KNOW IT DIDN'T REALLY HAVE NO MEANING AND JOY WITH

OUT THE LORD? DIDN'T YOU KNOW YOU NEEDED TO STOP AND LOOK BACK
BECAUSE THERE WAS SOMETHING YOU WERE MISSING?
YOU WERE MISSING JESUS. HE HAS BEEN IN FRONT OF YOU IN ALL YOUR TIMES,

## A MENTION AWAY AND A FOOTSTEP TO WALK (cont'd)

BUT YOU COULD NOT SEE HIM, AND HE HAS BEEN IN BACK OF YOU JUST BEFORE
THE FALL AND YOU STILL DID NOT SEE HIM OR HEAR HIS CALL.
BUT STILL HE HAS BEEN WATCHING, AND WAITING, SO STOP AND LOOK UP,
STOP AND LOOK BACK, STOP AND LOOK AROUND. JUST ONE TOUCH AND HE'LL SET
YOUR SOUL IN HIS SPIRIT AND YOU WON'T EVER HAVE TO LOOK AROUND AGAIN.
EVERYTHING YOU NEED WILL BE IN FRONT OF YOU, AND EVERYTHING
IS JUST A MENTION AWAY AND A FOOTSTEP TO WALK.
HE'LL PUT YOUR FOOTSTEPS IN HIS AND THIS OLD ROAD YOU'LL NEVER HAVE TO
WALK IT ALONE. ONLY IF YOU BELIEVE THAT JESUS IS JUST A MENTION
AND A FOOTSTEP TO WALK.

# WHAT IF?

YOU'RE MY ONCE IN A LIFETIME SECRET LOVE
AFFAIR THAT CAME FROM AFAR
AND TOUCHED MY VERY SOUL. SPOKEN THROUGH
THE EYES OF YOUR INNOCENCE I
TRULY BELIEVE THAT I TOUCHED YOUR SOUL TOO.
YESTERDAY IS BUT TOO FAR TO REMINENSE ABOUT
ALL THE BEAUTIFUL THINGS THAT WE
SHARED, WONDERING WHAT IF?
SO WHAT IF WE DID HAVE A SECRET LOVE AFFAIR,
AND PEOPLE COULD NOT SEE. AND,
WHAT IF WE HAD A SECRET LOVE AFFAIR AND THE
ONLY TWO PEOPLE TO SEE WERE YOU
AND I.
WHAT IF WE MADE LOVE ON THE 22ND FLOOR AND LET
THE MOONLIGHT CATCH OUR SOULS.
AND, WHAT IF, WE MADE LOVE FOR THE VERY FIRST
TIME AFTER MANY EPISODES OF WHAT
IF'S?
AND, WHAT IF OUR TIME SPENT TOGETHER WASN'T
JUST ABOUT MAKING LOVE, BUT WAS
SHARED BY GOING FOR LONG WALKS ON THE BEACH,
HOLDING HANDS AND HUGGING AND
KISSING WONDERING, WHAT IF?
AND, WHAT IF WE JUST TALKED AND MADE LOVE
WITHIN OUR SOULS AND IT WAS JUST
BETWEEN THE TWO OF US BECAUSE A SECRET LOVE
AFFAIR WE ARE.
AND, WHAT IF WE STILL NEVER TOLD A SOUL. AND,
WHAT IF WE NEVER STOPPED OUR
SECRET AND CONTINUED THIS LOVE AFFAIR TAKING
IT TO ANOTHER LEVEL AND ALWAYS
WITH THE QUESTION, WHAT IF?

# THE PUREST OF A RADIANT LOVE

SUPPOSE LOVE WAS ONLY FOR ONE MORE
DAY AND THAT DAY WAS TODAY? THEN I
WOULD BE BLESSED TO HAVE KNOWN LOVE WITH
YOU IN IT
AND I WOULD PRAY FOR ONE MORE DAY. IF A LOVE
BLESSING
CAME DOWN FROM THE GOOD LORD IN HEAVEN
ABOVE, I WOULD BE
BLESSED TO HAVE KNOWN A RADIANT LOVE WITH
YOU AND I IN IT.
PRAYING FOR YET ANOTHER DAY, I AM THANKFUL
AND I WOULD MAKE
EACH AND EVERY MOMENT ENDURED WITH LOVE,
EVERLASTING LOVE.
IT IS SEEN THROUGH KNOWING LOVE AND LOOKING
AT A LOVE THAT WE
CAN NO LONGER OPEN OUR EYES ONE AT A TIME AND
SAY LOVE TODAY,
BUT TOMORROW
YOU HAVE TO STAY IN AND BE SAFE.WHAT IS
TOMORROW,
ESPECIALLY WHENYOU OR NO ONE
HAS EVER LIVED IN IT.

## NO STRINGS ATTACHED

SPOKEN LIKE A PRO, FROM YOUR LIPS TO MINE,
NO STRINGS ATTACHED. FUNNY HOW IT SEEMS,
YOU REALLY THOUGHT YOU HAD IT GOING
ON! BUT FROM MY LIPS TO YOURS, A WHISPER
AND A WIMPER, AND IT ALL
WENT AWAY. I DIDNT TRY TO HOOK YOU,

I DIDNT EVEN THROW YOU MY BEST. I JUST LAID
BACK AND
ACTED LIKE WHO I AM, AND WHEN I
LOOKED BACK AT CHA, I HAD YOU HOOKED AND
YOU WERE MINE.FUNNY HOW IT SEEMS FROM MY
LIPS TO
YOURS, NO STRINGS ATTACHED.

# THE VACATION

THE WORLD IS BEAUTIFUL, THE WORLD IS BEAUTIFUL
AS I SPREAD MY WINGS, THE WORLD IS BEAUTIFUL AS
I FLY AWAY,
2 DAYS LEFT TILL I LEAP, JUMP, WAIT I'M THINKING
I'M SUPERWOMAN,
BUT WATCH ME FLY! I'M STARTING MY WEEK ON A
FANTASTIC NOTE
BECAUSE I'M SO HAPPY HOW THE WEEK WILL END! I
AM NOW STARTING
MY COUNT DOWN TIME AND I WILL BE COUNTING
AND SMILING AND
DAY DREAMING AND BECOMING MORE IMPATIENT AS
THE DAYS GO
BY. I'LL BE FLUTTERING WITH EXCITEMENT FILLED
WITH JOY RUNNING
OVER AS I BLOW THIS JOINT ON FRIDAY. I WILL
LEAVE THIS BUILDING LIKE
A STRANGER IN THE NIGHT AND RUNNING OUT LIKE
I'M ON FIRE. HAVE A
GREAT BIG LOVELY DAY

## SPECIAL

TODAY IS A SPECIAL DAY THAT THE ANGELS SUNG
TO ME AND THE BIRDS CHIRPEDAND THE FLOWERS
BLOOMED AND ALL THAT WAS SURROUNDING
LEAPED AND DANCED AND THE WORLD WAS HAPPY
AND
TODAY FELT SO SPECIAL

## JUST ONE MORE DAY

SOMETIMES WHEN I STOP AND THINK ABOUT WHAT I'VE SEEN
IN THIS LIFE, I WONDER WHY? BUT I'VE LEARN QUICKLY AND I STOPPED
QUESTIONING THE THINGS THAT MAKE THE WORLD GO ROUND AND
ROUND.  I SHOULDNT HAVE TIME TO THINK ABOUT THE THINGS THAT
MAKE ME FEEL BAD OR BUMMED OUT OR HAVE A LOOK THAT'S MAKING
EVERYBODY SAD. WAKE UP I TELL MYSELF, BE GLAD BECAUSE THIS TRUTH
SHALL PASS WITH EVERYTHING IN IT.  LAUGHTER, JOY, PEACE, AND THE
LOVE FOR ONE ANOTHER SHOULD BE THE PURPOSE OF A GOOD LIFE.
YOU DIDNT GET HERE BECAUSE MAN WANTED YOU HERE! IF YOU'D
JUST STOP AND THINK LONG ENOUGH YOU WOULD REALIZE THAT IT IS MAN
THAT DOESNT WANT YOU AROUND.  IT IS MAN THAT IS KILLING YOU FOR
NO APPARENT REASON.  IT IS JESUS WHO PLEADS WITH GOD
EVERYDAY FOR HIM TO GIVE HIM ANOTHER DAY SO THAT HE MAY
KEEP YOU HERE FOR JUST ONE MORE DAY.

# THIS OLD TREE

I AM THE TREE YOU PASS BY EVERY DAY OF YOUR
LIFE.
MY PURPOSE IS TO HELP YOU TO SURVIVE,
REMEMBER
I AM NOT THE ONE THAT NEEDS OXYGEN ON A
DAILY BASIS AND I AM NOT THE ONE THAT NEEDS
PAPER TO
WRITE WITH OR ANY OTHER PURPOSE I MIGHT SERVE
FOR YOU.
I DO NOT ABUSE YOU, SO WHY TRYAND ABUSE ME.
ONE DAY I, TOO, WILL GROW OLD AND THEN
WILL WE RUN A RACE TOGETHER TO SEE WHO WILL
CEASE
FIRST? SO LEAVE SOME OF MY ROOTS BEHIND LIKE
YOU
HAVE LEFT SOME OF YOURS BEHIND.BECAUSE IN THE
END
I WILL BE THE ONE TO LAST, LAST AND YOU WON'T
EVEN BE AT THE STARTING LINE NOR THE FINISHING
LINE, AND MY ROOTS WILL SPREAD WIDE AND HIGH,
AND
WHAT ABOUT YOU?

## RETIREMENT

RETIREMENT KNOWS THE PLEASURES OF A GREAT START AND ENDS WITH ENDLESS OPPORTUNITIES FOR GREAT BEGINNINGS.

## SOMETHING SO REAL

LOVE WAS THE THOUGHT BEFORE YOUR VISION OF THE PIECE THAT WAS MISSING, THAT SOMETHING, THAT SOMEONE.

LOVE IS THE LINK TO THE PUREST THING THAT GOD GAVE TO US, BUT YET IT IS THE HARDEST THING THAT TWO PEOPLE COULD EVER DO AND STILL BE ONE.

ACKNOWLEDGE HIS BLESSING AND SAY THANK YOU FOR ALL THINGS.
ACKNOWLEDGE HIS BLESSING AND SAY THANK YOU FOR ALL THINGS TO COME.

REMEMBER, THIS IS THE END OF THE PARTIAL, THE BEGINNING OF WHAT HAS BEEN MADE WHOLE, BECAUSE TODAY YOU CAN SAY, "WE ARE HERE AS ONE".

SO DON'T FORGET TONIGHT TO SAY A PRAYER BEFORE YOU LAY DOWN AS WE AND DON'T FORGET TO SAY A PRAYER BEFORE YOU RISE AS WE, AND WHEN YOU RISE DON'T FORGET TO SAY THANK YOU TO GOD AS YOU RISE TOGETHER AS ONE.

LOVE MADE YOU BOTH STEP OUT OF YOURSELVES AND RISE TOGETHER AS ONE. SO DON'T EVER LOOK BACK AT LOVE BECAUSE HERE IT IS AND IT STANDS IN FRONT OF YOU FOR BOTH YOUR EYES TO SEE. GOD NEVER MADE A MISTAKE WHEN HE GAVE YOU LOVE, HE GAVE YOU HIS LOVE FOR THE DAYS TO COME. WITH THE KNOWLEDGE THAT HE HAS GIVEN TO THE BOTH OF YOU, HE NOW GIVES TO YOU HIS LOVE AS

ONE. ONE LOVE, ONE UNITY AND ONE UNDERSTANDING. BY AND BY AND THROUGH IT ALL YOU WILL LOVE HIM FIRST AND THAT LOVE WILL CONTINUE TO FLOW OVER INTO YOUR LOVE FOR EACH OTHER REMEMBERING THAT THIS IS THE DAY THAT HE HAS GIVEN TO YOU TO BECOME A WHOLE IN EACH OTHER.

<u>SO IF SOMEONE WHERE TO ASK YOU, "WHAT IS LOVE TODAY?"</u>

IT IS THE BOTH OF YOU IN THE LIGHT.

IT IS THE VISION OF A MAN SEARCHING FOR A WOMAN.
IT IS THE VISION OF A WOMAN SEARCHING FOR A MAN.
IT IS THE VISION THAT ANY ONE MAN CAN HAVE,
IT IS THE VISION THAT ANY ONE WOMAN COULD HAVE.
IT IS THE TRUE MEANING THAT REAL DREAMS DO COME TRUE.

## NOTHING TO SOMETHING

LOVE IS NOT A BATTLE, NOR A STORM AND IT ISN'T SOMETHING FOR
NOTHING.
IT IS "YOUR" BATTLE OF NOTHINGS THAT KEEP YOU CAPTIVE AND IT IS
"YOUR STORM THAT LEADS YOU TO BELIEVE IT WILL BE OVER SOON.
LOVE IS ONE THING FOR SURE THAT WILL BE WHEN WE CAN LONGER BE.
IT STANDS FOR ALL THE THINGS YOU ARE, ALL THE THINGS THAT YOU WILL
BE, BUT IT IS NEITHER A BATTLE NOR A STORM, A WANT OR A NEED.
IT IS A NEW PLACE IN OUR HEARTS THAT WE ARE DEVELOPING. LIKE TINY
FEET OF A BABY TAKING IT'S FIRST STEPS, WE TOO ARE TRYING OUR
BEST.
SOMETHING MUST WE PUT BACK TURNING IT BACK INTO NOTHING,
UNLEASHING AND SYCHONIZING ALL THE NOTHINGS UNTIL ALL ARE REAL
SOMETHINGS.

# THE BONNER & NICHOLSON FAMILY REUNION

THIS IS THE REAL EXCITEMENT OF OUR REUNION BRINGING US CLOSER WITH HOPES OF SEEING AND MEETING NEW FACES NEVER SEEN BEFORE.

THIS IS THE GATHERING POINT OF A REUNION OF A FAMILY TOLD BY MANY FACES THAT CAME FROM MANY PLACES. EACH NEW FACE IS FOR THE EMPTY SPACE THAT USED TO BE.

WE CIRCLE OUR CHAIN WITH LINKS OF LOVE HOPING THAT THE ONES THAT AREN'T WITH US TODAY, WILL BE LINKED INSIDE THE CIRLE, SO THAT OUR LOVE IS LINKED INSIDE AND OUT.

THESE ARE OUR ROOTS, OUR FAMILY, AND OUR PEOPLE.
THESE ARE OUR MEMORIES OF ALL THE HUGS AND KISSES FROM ALL OF THE NEW AND OLD FACES THAT GAVE ALL OF THEIR LOVE.

OUR ROOTS, OUR PEOPLE, OUR FAMILY.

OUR UNION! LOOK AROUND, YOU SEE THIS IS OUR FAMILY, OUR FAMILY REUNION THAT IS BEING TOLD BY YOU, YOU, AND YOU OF SO MANY DIFFERENT FACES.

# DEFININITION OF STUPID

I WAS STUPID AND COULD NOT SEE PAST YOUR LIES.
THEN I WAS STUPID AGAIN,
AND I TRIED NOT TO SEE ALL OF YOUR LIES BUT NOW
I AM FOUND, I WAS BLIND,
NOW I CAN SEE RIGHT THROUGH ALL YOUR LIES.
THROUGH IT ALL YOU GAVE ME THE DEFINITION OF
STUPID, WHICH I WAS, AND NOW
I AM NOT.
YOU GAVE ME EYES TO SEE THE WICKEDNESS IN
YOUR LIES.  WHAT LYES BENEATH
MUST SURFACE.  SO NOW I MUST SEE WHO YOU
REALLY ARE AND WHO I REALLY AM
AND DEFINE THE WORD STUPID,I AM NOT.
STUPID DEFINES THAT ALL THINGS ARE POSSIBLE
AND IT'S POSSIBILITIES COULD
BE ENDLESS, BUT THEY ARE NOT, SO DEFINE TO ME
THIS ROLE OF STUPID BECAUSE
I HAVE SOMETHING YOU DON'T.  A HEART! STILL
PLAYING THOSE GAMES, I KNOW
WHO I AM, BUT CAN YOU DEFINE WHO YOU REALLY
ARE.

# REJECTED

YOU REJECTED OUR SOCIETY, SO YOU KILLED
OUR PEOPLE AND HID LIKE THE
COWARD YOU ARE.
WHEN DID YOU DETERMINE THAT HIS OR HER
LIFE WAS NOT WORTH LIVING?
DIDN'T YOU KNOW THAT LITTLE CHILDREN
WOULD LYE AWAKE AND CRY AND ASK
FOR THEIR MOMMIES AND DADDIES?
DIDN'T YOU KNOW THAT A MOTHER OR A
FATHER WHO HAD RAISED THEIR CHILDREN
WOULD ASK WHY?
DIDN'T YOU KNOW THAT THE BEST FRIEND
THAT I EVER HAD WOULDN'T BE SHARING
THEIR LAUGHTER, THEIR SMILE AND LOVE
WITH ME?
DIDN'T YOU KNOW THAT SOCIETY HAD NOT
REJECTED THEM, AND THAT THEY WERE
OURS, AND WE LOVED THEM? WHETHER OR
NOT WE KNEW THEM, THAT WAS NOT THE
QUESTION BECAUSE THEY WERE APART OF US
AND WE APART OF THEM LONG BEFORE
YOU DECIDED TO REJECT THEM.

## JUST GET ALONG

IF, FOR ONE DAY, WE ALL CRIED TOGETHER,
BUT CRIED AS ONE, WHY CAN'T WE
ALL JUST GET ALONG. IF FOR ONE DAY WE
COMFORTED EACH OTHER AND WE DID
THIS TOGETHER, AND WE DID IT FOR ALL,
THEN AGAIN, WE WERE AS ONE. TELL
ME, WHY CAN'T WE ALL JUST GET ALONG?
IF ALL OF THESE PEOPLE, TOGETHER AND AS
ONE, DIDN'T KNOW THEY WERE DYING
FOR US, AND DID JUST THAT, IMAGINE JESUS
DYING FOR ALL OF US, THAT WE
MIGHT BE AS ONE. THEN TELL ME WHY CAN'T
WE ALL LOVE ONE ANOTHER AND ALL
JUST GET ALONG?

## A GLIMPSE

THE DAY THE WORLD CRIED TOGETHER ALL
AT ONCE AS A GLIMPSE OF WHAT MIGHT.
THE FLIGHT THAT OPENED AND CAPTURED
THE SKIES WITH DISBELIEF. STILL A
GLIMPSE OF WHAT IF, WHAT MIGHT, AND
SADNESS FILLED THE WORLD AS DARKNESS
SPOKE, "TERROR IS AT HAND.
A GLIMSPE OF WHAT WAS, AND THE HEARTS
OF MANY GOOD OUTWEIGHTED THE HEARTS
OF THOSE WHO CREATED THIS EVIL. THE
SKIES OPENED UP AND WE FILLED
THE SKIES WITH ALL OF OUR HURT, OUR PAIN,
AND OUR DISBELIEF THAT
SOMETHING THIS BAD COULD HAPPEN AND WE
AS A PEOPLE NEVER KNEW IT COULD
HAPPEN TO US. EVEN THOUGH WE DID NOT
COME OUT WITH WHAT WE CAME IN WITH,
WE CAME OUT WITH A LITTLE BIT MORE.
JESUS WASN'T WRONG ABOUT US, BECAUSE
WE GATHERED IN HIS NAME AND ON THIS
DAY, IN THE MIDST OF TERROR, WE GAVE
LOVE AND WE GOT SOME BACK. WE CRIED
AS INDIVIDUALS BUT WE REALLY CRIED AS
ONE. THEY, THE VICTIMS, THEY DIED
AS INDIVIDUALS, BUT REALLY THEY DIED AS
ONE.

# I WONDER

I LAY AND WONDER WHY THE EVILS
SOMETIME SEEM TO BE TOO MUCH.
THE RIGHT THINGS TO DO TELL US THAT
THERE'S A BATTLE TO WALK, MANY WORDS
TO TALK AND TOO MANY TEARS TO SHED.
OUR HEARTS ARE LIKE CLOUDS OF WATER
AND STILL WE LAY AND WONDER WHY. THESE
EVILS WON'T GO AWAY BY
THEM SELVES, IT IS UP TO US TO CLAIM THE
VICTORY.
SO FOR EVERY LIFE THAT MUST FIGHT THE
BATTLE AND FOR EVERY LIFE THAT HAS
FOUGHT THE BATTLE, WE AS GOD'S PEOPLE
MUST TAKE A STAND. WE CAN NOT
REPLACE THE ONE'S THAT HAVE LEFT, BUT WE
STILL MUST NOT LET EVIL FILL
THE VOID AND INSTEAD LET THE LOVE GROW
TO FILL A VOID OR TWO, AND KEEP
KEEPING ON.

## NO WORDS

I KNOW IN MY HEART THAT REAL HEARTS
CRIED OUT LOUD FOR ALL THE
VICTIMS THAT WERE BRUTALLY MASACRED.
HOW CAN I EXPLAIN BRUTAL OR EVEN THE
WORD MASACRE. THERE'S NO
DEFINITION TO EXPRESS; NO REASONING. THIS
COULD NOT BE THE ACT
OF GOD'S PEOPLE BECAUSE I KNOW DEEP
DOWN INSIDE HE CRIED TOO.

## THIS IS OUR VICTORY

THERE'S SO MUCH TO TELL, FOR OUR YOUNG
AND OLD EYES HAVE SEEN THE
DESTRUCTION OF THE COMING OF MAN.
QUIET YOUR HEARTS AND EARS BECAUSE IT
WON'T BE TOO LONG TILL ALL THAT IS
BAD HAS BEEN MADE GOOD.
SO PLOT YOUR WARS AGAINST US BECAUSE
YOU WON'T SUCEED. KILL OUR
MOTHERS, FATHERS, SISTERS, BROTHERS AND
WHOMEVER ELSE YOU CAN BECAUSE YOU
STILL WON'T SUCCEED.
QUIETLY YOU WILL THINK YOU HAVE
VICTORY BUT AGAIN YOU DON'T. WE ARE AS
ONE AND AS A WHOLE WE CLAIM THE
VICTORY.

# HISTORY

PEOPLE WALK, THEY DON'T FLY.
BUILDINGS ARE BUILT HIGH, HERE TODAY,
GONE TOMMOROW, HOW DO WE SAY
BYE, BYE.
WHY ARE WE LOOKING AT A PICURE WITH NO
EYES?
WHY, OH WHY, MUST WE CONTINUE TO DIE.

# MAN

MAN WAS NOT MADE TO STAND ALONE NOR
THROW STICKS AND STONES!

## THANK YOU

I DIDN'T GET A CHANCE TO THANK YOU, BUT I
KNOW DEEP DOWN INSIDE
YOU HEARD ME IN YOUR HEART.
SO THANK YOU FOR BEING MY GREATEST
HERO AND THANK GOD FOR HIM SENDING
YOU TO ME AND THANK GOD FOR ME
REALIZING THAT GOD'S HELPER'S THEY COME,
AND THEY COME RIGHT ON TIME. SO THANK
YOU GOD AND THANK YOU FOR HAVING
ONE OF YOUR HELPER'S AROUND SO THAT I
WOULD NOT BE LEFT ALONE.

## STATISTICS

I WASN'T INCLUDED IN THIS YEAR'S
STATISTICS BUT I WAS MURDURED ANYWAY.
YOU DIDN'T KNOW ME, AND YOU DIDN'T EVEN
CARE.
MY FELLOW AMERICANS DIDN'T KNOW ME
BUT THEY DID INDEED CARE AND THEY
CRIED FOR ME ANYWAY.
LIKE A THIEF, I WAS STOLEN AWAY AND TO
NEVER BE RETURNED. LIKE THE
FLAMES WITNESSED THE FIRE OF LIFE SHOULD
NEVER DISAPPEAR.
MY LIFE IS SPREAD ALL OVER YOURS, SO LET
THE FLAMES BE BRIGHT AND NOT
BURN IN DARKNESS.
LIFE IS NOT IN VEIN. IT IS THE NOT DOING
THAT MAKES US LIVE IN VEIN.
MY DARKNESS IS IN THE LIGHT THAT SHINES
FOR ALL OF LIFE'S POSSIBILITIES THAT STRIVE
TO
SUCCEED IN THIS VICTORY OF THIS FIGHT.

# RUN

A SKY FULL OF DARKNESS, IT WAS RUNNING
FASTER THAN I.
WHITE, CHALKY AND CHOKING BLACK, LIKE
NOTHING NO ONE HAS
EVER SEEN.
FEAR, GRASPING, TRYING TO HOLD ME BACK,
AND FAITH KEEPING ME
MOVING. IT SAID, "RUN AND RUN FAST.

## THANK ME LATER

RUN FAST AND THANK ME LATER,
INDEED YOU'LL DO JUST THAT.
RUN AND RUN FAST!
I WILL GIVE YOU A PATH.
RUN AND RUN FASTER.
REMEMBER, I'LL NEVER LEAVE YOUR SIDE
AND
IF YOU SHOULD FALL I'LL BE YOUR
FEET AND I'LL RUN EVEN FASTER.

# TEACH

TEACH YOUR HEART NOT TO BE HARD, BUT BE
GENTLE AND STRONGLY HEARD.
TEACH YOUR HEART NOT TO BE BLIND, BUT TO
SEE THAT TEMPTATION IS
DESTRUCTION.
DESTRUCTION IS FELT ALL THE DAYS YOU
HAVE NO HEART. LOVE AND LOVING
GOD MAKES US NOT BLIND, BECAUSE HE HAS
STOOD BY, WATCHED AND GAVE
US EYES TO NOW SEE.

# CUT SHORT

“WHEN I GROW UP I
WANNA????????????????????????????????

CUT SHORT, YOU SEE, I NEVER GOT THE
CHANCE TO BECOME THE
PERSON I WAS REALLY MEANT TO BE.

MOMMY!!!!!!!!!!DADDY!!!!!!!!!!!!!!!!!
I NEVER GOT A CHANCE TO HEAR THOSE
WORDS.

DA DA DA!!!!!!!!!!!!!!!!!!!!!!
I DIDN’T EVEN GET TO COME HERE AND START
LIFE.

I LOVE YOU!!!!!!!!!!!!!!!!!!!!!!!!
I WAS TOO YOUNG TO REALLY KNOW WHAT IT
REALLY MEANT.
I WAS TOO YOUNG TO SAY MY FIRST WORDS
AND WALK MY FIRST
STEPS.

GOOD BYE!!!!!!!!!!!!!!!!!!!!!!!!1

I JUST THOUGHT, WELL,……I NEVER GOT A
CHANCE TO SAY THOSE WORDS EITHER.

## SPREAD WORLDWIDE

IF PEACE WERE SPREAD WORLDWIDE,
THEN IN MY HEART MY GOD WOULD
BE HAPPY AND EVERY DAY WOULD BE
SUNDAY AND PAIN AND SUFFERING
WOULD CEASE TO EXIST.
I CALL HIM MY GOD BECAUSE IF YOU
HAD HIM IN YOUR HEARTS, YOU WOULD CALL
HIM YOUR GOD TOO, AND PEACE WOULD BE
SPREAD WORLDWIDE.

## GIVE

LOVE IS LIKE A DISEASE
SHOW SOME AND LET IT SPREAD.

# DESTRUCTION

SELL YOUR HEARTS, NOT YOU'RE SOULS.
TAKE PRIDE AND BE SELF-SUFFICIENT
IN KNOWING WHAT GOD HAS PROVIDED FOR
US.
DESTRUCTION IS INSUFFICIENT. IT TAKES AND
TAKES AND TAKES AND SOON THERE'S
NOTHING
LEFT TO TAKE.
BE SOFT BUT STRONG AND FIRM IN THE
WORDS
YOU PASS ALONG THE WAY. DESTRUCTION
DOES NOT KNOW WHOSE IN IT'S WAY.
LAY YOUR PATH THE RIGHT WAY BECAUSE
DESTRUCTION RUNS FASTER AND WHEN WERE
NOT
LOOKING, IT TAKES US BY SURPRISE.

## FREE

BEAUTIFUL AS WAVES THAT RUSH IN AS ARE
THE WATERS THAT SEE CLEAR
AND THE FLOWERS THAT BLOOM FROM AFAR
WATCHING THE EYES AMAZEMENT.
STILL, BREATH TAKING AS I PARTAKE,
FULLFILLING AS FOOD
CONSUMED, BEAUTIFUL I AM INDEED,
BEAUTIFUL I AM, I AM FREEDOM AS IT
RISES UP AND FLOWS THRU.

# JUST BEING ME

I'M LIKING WHAT I SEE, ALL OF ME, AND I'M
TAKING WHAT DESTINY HAS BROUGHT
TO ME, AND I'M JUST BEING ME.
I'M LIKING WHAT I SEE & WHO I AM, I'M
LOOKING AND I'M SEEING THE
BEAUTIFUL BLACK BEAUTY I AM. I'M FEELING
GOOD EVERYDAY BECAUSE
I'M FEELING AND LIKING WHAT I SEE.

## THE PRETENDER

I AM A PRETENDER WAITING FOR MY MOMENT,
MY AUDIENCE.
I AM A PRETENDER, WILL YOU BELIEVE WHAT
YOU SEE, AND WILL YOU BELIEVE ME?
I AM A PRETENDER OF THE PAST WAITING TO
SEE YOU HERE IN THE FUTURE.
WILL YOU SEE WHAT I SEE, WILL YOU HEAR
WHAT I HEAR, WILL YOU DO AS I DO?

# FROM AFAR

WHEN I DIDN'T KNOW YOU, YOU WATCHED ME
FROM AFAR. I DID NOT KNOW
THIS THEN AND I DO NOT KNOW YOU NOW.
IT WAS A WORD OR TWO THAT YOU SPOKE
THAT MADE ME WONDER.
CURIOSITY REVEALS POSSIBLITIES AND IN THE
EVENT I NO LONGER WONDER
IT'S ALL BECAUSE I KNOW YOU NOW.

# INSCRIPTIONS

THE INSCRIPTION OF INFATUATION DESCRIBES
ITSELF AS BEING LIGHT AS
A FEATHER, STORMY AS NORTH CAROLINA'S
BAD WEATHER AND AS SWEET AS
REALIZING YOU WEREN'T IN LOVE WITH THAT
PERSON AFTER ALL.

## NOT THE FREAK

I AM NOT THE FREAK!
I'M JUST LAID BACK, STRONG BUT NOT WEAK.
I AM JUST ME, DOING ME.
WHAT I AM IS WHO I AM. I DON'T SPEAK LOUD,
I SPEAK FREE. I AM PRIVATE, I AM QUIET, I AM
ME,
JUST DOING ME. QUIET LOVELY I AM, STILL I
AM NOT
THE FREAK.

# SEARCH

SEARCH FOR MY LOVE
IN YOUR HEART,
IT'S THERE, DON'T YOU SEE IT.
MY HEART IS NOT BLIND, IT BLENDS
WITH THE SOFTNESS OF RHYTHM DANCING WITH
RHYMES.I THOUGHT I TOUCHED YOUR HEART AS OUR
SOULS ENTWINDED AS WE WERE EMBRACED BY THE
UNKNOWN.

## LESS THAN SATISFIED

WHY DO YOU SELL YOUR BODIES FOR LESS
SATISFACTION, AND NO
GRATIFICATION? WHY DO YOU DRESS UP AND
HANG OUT LIKE DROVES

OF CATTLE WAITING FOR THE WEAK AND THE
WEAKEST.
BY THE CURVESIDE YOU WORK IT LIKE A FREAK
FOR
A WOMAN OR A MAN WHOSE MIND AND BODIES
ARE XRAYED AS
JUNKIES WAITING TO GET THAT FIX. WHETHER
YOU ENHALE A WOMANS PART
OR GIVE IT TO THE MAN BLOW BY BLOW, YOUR
STILL THE NEXT FIX. YOUR
THE COMMENTATOR GIVING IT TO THEM BLOW BY
BLOW HITTING YOU RIGHT
IN THE MOUTH. STILL, I DO NOT KNOW WHY YOU
INSIST THE UNKOWN
OCCUPY THE KNOWN AND THEN MOVE ON TO THE
NEXT. IT'S BEEN A GOOD
NIGHT, NEXT!

# WHEN IT'S OVER

WHEN IT'S OVER, SOUND THE GAVEL, CAUSE YOU GET'S NO
SATIFACTION HERE! SOUND THE GAVEL AND KEEP DARN WALKING,
YOU'LL BE WARNED ONLY ONCE. DON'T TURN BACK, BECAUSE
WHEN IT'S OVER, IT OVER, THE GAVEL HAS SOUNDED SAYING THIS CASE CLOSED,
NEXT!

## WASTE NOT!

DON'T WASTE MY TIME, ROOKIE THINKING YOUR
GETTING
AWAY WITH A LITTLE SOMETHING, SOMETHING. YOU
SEE,
I PEEKED YOUR GAME FROM THE FORTUNE COOKIE
AND GOT
ZERO.

# FRAMED AND POISED

BEAUTY WAS IN FRONT OF ME.
BEAUTY WAS ON THE SIDE OF ME.
IT WAS STANDING AND WAITING ALL
AROUND ME. THEN I REACHED AND
REALIZED BEAUTY WAS ALL INSIDE ME.
THAT'S THE BEAUTY OF TRUTH.
NEVER DID I IMAGINE THAT TRUTH WAS
PART OF MY DESTINY TO MY BEAUTY WHICH
ALLOWED ME TO BE, AND TRANSFORMED ME FREE
TO BE JUST ME. I FOUND A BEAUTIFUL BLACK
ME, FRAMED AND POISED.

# WHO ARE YOU?

AWAKENED FROM THIS DREAM I AM DRIPPING WET,
AND
SCARY AS IT SEEMS, IT'S NOT.
EVERY NIGHT I'M DREAMING THIS DREAM, AND I'M
NOT
SEEING YOUR FACE.
CURIOUS IN MY OWN DREAM, I WAIT TO FALL ASLEEP
AND THEN MAYBE I'LL SEE YOUR FACE.

# FULLFILLED

SURPRISING AS EXCELLERATING,
EXCELLERATING AS REFRESHING,
REFRESHING AS TASTEFUL,
TASTEFUL AS CAPTIVATING,
CAPTIVATING AS CAPTURING ONE'S
REAL DESIRE.

## THE WALLS OF LOVE

BENEATH THE WALLS OF LOVE YOU FOUND TRUTH,
NOT HARD TO SEE, NOT EVEN HARD TO FEEL.
JUST FOOLING AROUND AND BEING FRIENDS, TRUTH
WAS INSPIRED AND A STORY WAS TOLD. WE DIDN'T
DRESS UP
AND IMMITATE A FAIRY TALE, BUT THE FAIRY TALE
CAME
TRUE. IMPELLING IT WAS, BENEATH THE WALLS OF
LOVE
IT'S NOT SO HARD TO SEE.

## TOO MUCH FOR ONE TO BEAR

WHAT'S BETWEEN YOU AND I, IS FOR ONLY YOU AND I TO SEE.
SEEING THE WAYS OF THE WORLD AT A GLANCE WOULD BE
TOO MUCH FOR ONE PERSON TO SEE OR BEAR. SO SEE NOT THE WAYS OF
THE WORLD, BE NOT OF THE WORLD, BUT BE ABOUT THE WORLD
CHANGING THE WAYS OF THE WORLD CHANGING THE WAYS THAT MAKE
US STRUGGLE WITHOUT CAUSE AND LEAD US TO BELIEVE
THERE IS NO WAY OUT.

# ALL ELSE

CHEER YOU HEARTS WITH FAITH KNOWING IT WILL
STAND
WHEN ALL ELSE FALLS.

# REVENGE

YOU SAY YOU'RE UPTIGHT BECAUSE TWO WRONGS DIDN'T
MAKE IT RIGHT AND YOUR WAITING BECAUSE SOONER OR
LATER, IT'S OUT OF SIGHT OUT OF MIND.
YOU CALL OUT, I'M GONNA GET YOU SUCKER, AND SOON
OUT OF SIGHT AND OUT OF MIND, REVENGE. SIGHT AND MIND
IS OUT OF SIGHT AND REVENGE IS BLOOD RUSHING, OOH
THIS FEELS SO GOOD, SO RIGHT, DAMN, MY CONSCIOUS IS
HERE, IT'S IN SIGHT, I CAN SEE IT, IT CAN SEE ME TOO.
MY BLOOD RUSHING IS COMING DOWN, THIS AINT'T RIGHT
AND I'M UPTIGHT BECAUSE TWO WRONGS REALLY DIDN'T MAKE
IT RIGHT

## NOT LONG

YOU SAY YOU WANNA LIVE A LONG LIFE JUST LIKE
ME,
BE LIKE ME, AND LIVE LIFE LONG. BUT CAN YOU LIVE
LIFE
LOVED, WILL YOU GET LOST IN THIS LIFE OR WILL
YOU WEAR
A VEIL WITH LIFE RUNNING LONG, LIFE RUNNING
STRONG.
I CAN'T RUN THE RACE FOR YOU, BUT, IF YOU RUN
ALONG SIDE
ME, MAYBE, JUST MAYBE WHEN WE GET THERE
WE'LL GET THERE
TOGETHER. LIFE IS LIKE A MARRIAGE, FOR BETTER
OR WORSE,
IN SICKNESS AND HEALTH, TILL DEATH DO US PART?
CAN YOU FIND YOUR WAY OR CAN WE AS PEOPLE
FIND LIFE TOGETHER?
REMEMBER, YOU SAID YOU WANTED TO BE JUST LIKE
ME.

## ONE MAN AND FOUR WOMEN

I SEE ONE MAN AND FOUR WOMEN, FOUR LIES AND THREE
WOMEN HOLDING ON TO ONE LIE.
ONE MAN'S HOLDING THE BLAME FOR THREE WOMEN IN SHAME.
ONE DAME JUMPED OUT WHILE ANOTHER JUMPED IN, STILL NO ONE'S TO BLAME.
A DOLLAR AND A DEED THREE WOMEN IN NEED AND THE
FOURTH WOMAN INDEED PLAYS THE GAME WELL.
MAKES ONE MAN SCREAM BECAUSE HE KNOWS AND BELIEVES SHE'S
THE BLAME THAT HE HOLDS HIS HEAD IN SHAME. SHE'S THE
ONE HE CAN'T HAVE, STILL NO ONE'S TO BLAME UNTIL HE
REALIZES HE AINT GOT GAME, HE JUST GOT PLAYED FOR
ALL THREE WOMEN HE LEFT IN SHAME.

## FINGERTIPS

TOUCH MY FINGERTIPS BEFORE YOU SIP AND KISS
ALL
OVER MY LIPS.
FREE YOU MIND BEFORE YOU GET HERE BECAUSE
SOMETIMES
THINGS GET IN THE WAY.
IF THE MIND IS FREE, THEN THE BODY IS FREE TO
FOLLOW.

# APRIL

I WANT TO RUN FREE IN THE MORNING BLIST,
BLAZE LIKE SUN RAYS AND GROW AND BLOOM
LIKE MAY'S FLOWER. I WANT TO FEEL LIFE
LIKE APRIL'S SHOWER'S.

## SLIP INTO YOUR SOUL

IF YOU COULD ALMOST GET HERE IN MY MIND AND
SOUL WITH ME, I'D TAKE YOU THE REST OF THE WAY.
IF YOU COULD EVER BELIEVE THAT TWO PEOPLE
COULD
MAKE LOVE BEFORE THEY EVEN GOT THERE, THEN
BE
AMAZED AND BELIEVE AND IMAGINE WHAT THE
OUTCOME WOULD BE.
LET ME SLIP INTO YOUR SOUL FIRST AND AFTER
THAT I AM SURE THAT YOU WILL WANT TO JOIN ME
AND SLIP INTO MINE.

# THE VERGE

I HEAR THE FLOW OF RIGHTEOUSNESS BENEATH AND DEEP
DOWN IN MY SOUL. ON THE VERGE THE FLOW ALMOST STOLE
MY SOUL. AWAKENED AND STARTLED I QUICKLY VANISHED YOUR WORDS
AND HEARD MY KINDNESS THAT WAS BURIED. AS I HEARD
YOUR FOOTSTEPS THEY SCURRIED, TRYING TO SEARCH AND
FIND THE RIGHTEOUS WORD THAT ONCE AGAIN, MIGHT CONTAIN ME.
I HEARD AND I SAW THE LUCKY ME THAT WASN'T SO LUCKY.
SO AS I JOURNEY, I WANT YOU TO PREACH ON, PREACH TO ME, BUT,
DON'T TRY TO TAP MY SOUL. I'VE HEARD THE WORDS OF
CONTRIDICTION, I'VE SEEN THE WORDS THAT UNDERMINE ME AND
I KNOW THE SOUL THAT VANDELIZED MY SOUL. SO GO THERE WITH
ALL YOU GOT BECAUSE I WANT YOU TO KNOW, I WANT YOU TO
HEAR AND I WANT YOU TO SEE THESE FOOTSTEPS AS THEY
EMBRACE; EMBARK OUT OF THE DARK AND INTO THE SPARKLING LIGHT.

# MAKING LOVE

MAKING LOVE IS ONE ADVENTURE, KNOWING WHAT TO DO
WHEN YOU GET THERE IS ANOTHER, BUT THE HARDEST
IS WAITING FOR YOU TO GET HERE.

## IF YOU SEE ME

IF YOU SEE ME WALKING DOWN THE STREET THINK ABOUT ALL THE GOOD TIMES WE HAD, SOME WERE SAD, MANY WERE GLAD BUT NEVER DID WE GET MAD. SO REMEMBER ALL THE GOOD TIMES WE HAD.

ASHLEIGH CAONI JALIZA MARTIN
(DAUGHTER: AGE 8)

## SEE YOU

SEE YOU SOON, WHILE WE WAIT NOT KNOWING
WHAT WILL
HAPPEN TO US. SEE YOU SOON, WHILE WE RUN
AROUND
TRYING TO MAKE LIFE HAPPEN, DIDN'T YOU KNOW
THAT
IT HAD HAPPENED? SEE YOU SOON, ESPECIALLY
WHEN
YOU ARE NOT LOOKING, WHILE YOUR WAITING
AND NOT KNOWING WHAT AND WHEN IT WILL
HAPPEN. SO
I GUESS I'LL SEE YOU SOON.

# RAINING

THE RAIN WASHES THINGS CLEAN, IT WASHES THEM FREE.
UNLIKE PEOPLE WHEN THEY WASH CLEAN AND SEEM FREE,
THEY ARE NOT TRULY FREE.
IT IS ONLY WHEN YOU DECIDE THAT PEOPLE ARE PEOPLE, AND
IT IS GOD WHOM WILL WASH YOU CLEAN AND SET YOUR SPIRIT FREE.

# ONLY FOR A MOMENT

I CLOSED MY EYES AND RESTED OVER NIGHT. I DIDN'T KNOW THAT
THE REST I HAD HAD THE NIGHT BEFORE WOULD BE THE LAST PEACEFUL
SLEEP I WOULD ENCOUNTER FOR AWHILE.
I NEVER THOUGHT THAT IT WOULD ONLY BE FOR A MOMENT
TO HAVE PEACE LEAVE MY HEART, BUT, SOON I LAID AND ASKED THE LORD
TO RESTORE MY PEACE FROM WHICH HE HAD GAVE TO ME ONCE BEFORE.
THIS COULD NOT BE HAPPENING TO OUR WORLD, BUT IT HAD AND I
UNDERSTAND IT NOW. THIS HERE PLACE DOESN'T BELONG TO US.
WE ARE ONLY HERE TO SEE THE LAST MAN STANDING.

# PATIENCE

PATIENCE IS VIRTUE.
PATIENCE IS BEING BLESSED.

# MY KIDS

I FEEL AS THOUGH I AM SPECIAL,
NEVER WAS AN AUNT, YOU CALLED ME
YOUR AUNT ANYWAY, AND I AM SO GRATEFUL.
HAVING ALWAYS THOUGHT OF MYSELF AS
SOMEONE'S AUNT SPECIAL IN MY HEART
THIS WORD WAS TRULY FELT. THEN YOU
GUYS APPEARED IN MY LIFE AND FORTUNE AGAIN,
I WAS BLESSED AGAIN, AND AGAIN.
LOVE IS STOWED AWAY, AND ALWAYS HAVING SOME
LEFT OVER FOR THE ONE'S WHO COME LATE, BUT
ON TIME IN ONE'S LIFE MAKES AN ARRAY
OF LOVE BEAUTIFUL IN THE EYES THAT BEHOLD.

## ANDRE AND ASHLEIGH

I LOVE YOU FROM THE EAST AND WEST AND
FROM THE NORTH AND SOUTH AND INSIDE AND OUT.
FROM THE TOP OF MY HEART TO THE BOTTOM OF THE
BOTTOM OF MY HEART BECAUSE YOU ARE MY TWO
BEST
LINKS, AS I AM LINKED FROM MY MOM AND DAD.

# STELLA

STELLA DID GET HER GROVE BACK, BUT WHEN?

STELLA HAS ALWAYS BEEN GETTING HERE GROVE
ON,
THE GROVE WAS INVENTED BY HER AND INTENDED
FOR YOU, THE MAN. HAVE YOU EVER NOTICED
THAT THE TASTE IS SWEETER AND THE LOVE IS
WORTH COMING BACK TO, OVER AND OVER AGAIN.
AN ADDICTION TO THE BODY AND WHAT IT FEELS.
YOU WANNA TELL SOMEBODY, BUT SHE INSISTS NOT
TO.
STELLA YOU HAVE BEEN AROUND, SEEN A LOT, AND
STILL PEOPLE INSIST ON SAYING HOW STELLA GOT
HER
GROVE ON. IT'S STELLA LETTING YOU GET YOU
FREAK ON,
LEAVING YOU TO FIGURE OUT AND REMEMBER FOR
THE NEXT TIME
HOW YOU DID IT AND HOW YOUR GONNA DO IT.
SEE, THAT'S WHY THEY CALL STELLA,
STELLA. YOU GOT A STELLA GROVE AND I BET YOU
WON'T TELL A THANG

# ABOUT THE AUTHOR

I was raised in Freehold, New Jersey and served in the United States Army and Army Reserves for a total of eleven years. I refer to myself as a Plain-Jane kind of woman, nothing is fancy about me, though I appear shy, I am shy. I love family activities; I love loving my family and them loving me. Most people say they like the fine things in life, I generally like the simpler things in life. My finer things are things I wouldn't have any other way, like, my family, and the love you share together.

In my spare time I like to create crafts for gifts and I like to play bingo.

BINGO!!

www.ingramcontent.com/pod-product-compliance
Ingram Content Group UK Ltd.
Pitfield, Milton Keynes, MK11 3LW, UK
UKHW040016200726
13854UKWH00001B/237

9 780759 684096